When an inner situation is not made conscious,
it appears outside as fate.

Carl Jung

I thought about one of my favorite Sufi poems,
which says that God long ago
drew a circle in the sand
exactly around the spot
where you are standing right now.
I was never not coming here.
This was never not going to happen.

Elizabeth Gilbert

There's nowhere you can be
that isn't where you're meant to be...

John Lennon

Live in Love Fatebook

7 Empowering Ways to Thrill Your Heart,

Fuel Your Spirit, and Honor Your Soul

Edited by Lani Voivod

Contributors include: Christina Alexa, Kelly Lang, Kate Lemay,

Roderick Russell, Jenna Paige Sarno, Allen Voivod, and Lani Voivod

This book is dedicated to the passionate seekers, daring adventurers, resilient dreamers, and inspiring souls who have interrupted their lives, overcome odds, and shown up to join us at the Live in Love Retreat. Your open hearts and willing spirits have had a profound impact on all of our lives. Thank you for having the courage to say, "Yes!" to the little voice inside of you, for sharing your truth, and for bringing the magic of Sandy Island back to the mainland.

Ironically, the invitation to truly Live in Love is not for the faint of heart. You heard the call, and you answered it. This is a miracle.

<u>You</u> are a miracle.

Honor the miracle!

CONTENTS

Fate [feyt]

noun

1. something that unavoidably befalls a person; fortune; lot:
It is always his fate to be left behind.

2. the universal principle or ultimate agency by which the order of things is presumably prescribed; the decreed cause of events; time:
Fate decreed that they would never meet again.

3. that which is inevitably predetermined; destiny:
Triumph is our ineluctable fate.

4. a prophetic declaration of what must be:
The oracle pronounced their fate.

5. **the Fates**, Classical Mythology. the three goddesses of destiny, known to the Greeks as the Moerae and to the Romans as the Parcae.

verb (used with object), fated, fating.

6. to predetermine, as by the decree of fate; destine (used in the passive):
a person who was fated to be the savior of the country.

CHAPTER 1

1...2...3...

INITIATE YOUR FATE!

BY LANI VOIVOD

How does a book end up in your hands?

Does a friend give it to you? Do you order it from Amazon? Is it foisted upon you at an event, workshop, or retreat?

Maybe you notice it on your Mom's bedside table, in your neighbor's bathroom, or tossed in a pile at a local coffee shop. Something about it catches your eye, tickles your fancy. The title, cover art, a complimentary Facebook post, a person reading it at the beach, on a train, in a waiting room.

You sense the urge to pick it up. Pages flip past your thumb, and you feel the breeze of the paper flying by. You stop on a whim, take a peek at a random passage.

You decide then and there if this relationship will move to the next phase.

This dance of casual curiosity might be a simple coincidence. A way to pass time. A daydreamy habit of impulse and circumstance, hardly worth mentioning.

Or maybe – *just maybe* – it's **fate**.

THE SWEET L'IL NUDGE OF DESTINY

If you scan the highlight reel of your life, chances are the best moments and years that delight the mind weren't exactly planned. A series of events had to occur to deliver out-of-the-ordinary feelings, unusual opportunities, unexpected connections.

It is exactly this type of magic we – the seven friends and contributors of this book – hope to deliver to you.

As your humble companions and idea sherpas on this wild trek called life, please be advised we wear (and have worn) a heck of a lot of hats between us.

Your journey through the next 100 or so pages of this book will have you mingling minds, sparking synapses, and exchanging energy with:

- A world class sword swallower, mentalist, hypnotist, fire eater, entertainer, and expert in human potential

- 4 yoga teachers
- A globe-trotting singer/songwriter/musician
- 1 Executive Director with the world's largest nonprofit organization
- 4 small business owners
- The world's only daily Star Wars podcaster
- 2 certified nutritionists and wellness coaches
- 1 prolific painter and Artist of Conscious Evolution
- 2 veteran fire walkers
- 1 seasoned sweat lodge builder and sacred ceremony facilitator
- 5 Reiki practitioners and intuitive healers
- 1 legacy woodworker
- 2 social media and content marketing consultants
- 1 extreme rock climber with Mount Everest Base Camp bragging rights
- Several published authors, bloggers, public speakers, and professional catalysts
- 5 proud mothers
- 1 smitten newlywed
- 1 sassy, swingin' single
- 1 awesome dad

We are also, all of us, passionate seekers and compassionate dreamers; living, breathing testaments of imperfection and resurrection, emboldened actions and circadian distractions.

Like you, we all just want to **love and be loved**.

Feel good more often than we feel bad.

Learn tools and techniques that will make us healthier, smarter, braver, stronger, kinder, lighter, and wiser.

Laugh more, moan and groan less.

Experience the world with grace and wonder, joy and reverence.

Dare to **explore** our potential, **expand** our possibilities, and **embrace** our most vibrant, succulent opportunities.

Show up in our lives and relationships with an open heart, an enthusiastic mind, and a willing spirit.

More than anything, we all just want to **make peace** with who we are, **honor our gifts**, and **share the best we have to offer** with those who want or need it.

If that sounds like your cup of tea, then cuddle up, hunker down, and **enjoy this fun, fated invitation to live in love.**

We're excited for you!

Love,

Allen, Christina, Jenna, Kate, Kelly, Lani, and Roderick

Validate [val-i-deyt]

verb (used with object), validated, validating.

1. to make valid; substantiate; confirm.

2. to give legal force to; legalize.

3. to give official sanction, confirmation, or approval to, as elected officials, election procedures, documents, etc.: to validate a passport.

4. recognize or affirm the validity or worth of (a person or their feelings or opinions); cause (a person) to feel valued or worthwhile.

CHAPTER 2

VALIDATE

BY KATE LEMAY

I'm writing this in early April, two months away from the Live in Love Retreat. This is my fourth year co-hosting this transformational weekend experience on Lake Winnipesaukee's Sandy Island in New Hampshire. Each year, my co-founders and I choose a word to teach (and to learn!). This word becomes the theme of the workshop we each deliver to our Retreat guests, and it also inevitably becomes a theme in our lives, hearts, and happenings. We all joke that ultimately, the word we choose actually finds us, whether we like it or not. This year was no exception.

This is how I came to vexingly obsess about the word VALIDATE.

For months the aggravation simmered, creeping a degree or two hotter each week. The more I thought about the word VALIDATE - played with it, meditated on it, poked it, prodded it, and tried like heck to find peace with it - the more I really, *really* disliked it. So I did what any progress-yearning pragmatist dealing with a deadline would do. I started looking at my theme word from a safe, depersonalized, emotion-free distance.

VALIDATE: PERSPECTIVES FROM THE BLEACHERS

How do we make something valid? How do we substantiate and confirm it?

One way is through others. When people say things to you like:

"You look great, are you losing weight?"
"You seem to be so on top of things!"
"I'd love to join you/ spend time with you."

We appreciate the kind words, and often carry the positive feedback with us well beyond the interaction.

Another way we experience a sense of validation is through actions we do for ourselves, validating our own goals and objectives or proving what we know about ourselves. Running a marathon, getting a college degree, publishing a book, joining a steering committee, volunteering for a good cause – these are actions we take to feel a sense of pride or accomplishment, and to allow our time and efforts to be seen, honored, and hopefully appreciated by ourselves and others.

We assign the task of validation to so many fascinating things! Sometimes we use society's favorite tools of assessment, like scales, tape measures, clothes, the numbers in our bank accounts, the décor of our surroundings...

Other times, we get creative with our quest for confirmation, processing through journaling, crafting vision boards, getting our tarot cards read, participating in cultural or religious rituals, visiting palm readers, intuitives, energy healers, and even seeking feedback via my favorite inanimate counselor: a mood-tracking, customizable, ever-wise hormone app that lives on my phone.

We "legalize" things all the time. We validate and confirm all the time. So why oh why was I still feeling such steel-hearted resistance around this innocuous, three-syllabled word?

Then it hit me.

I may have participated in countless acts of validation over the years, but I have never really done it so consciously, with my eyes (and heart!) wide open.

Until now.

VALIDATE: PERSPECTIVES FROM THE PLAYING FIELD

Up until this point, my automatic reaction has been to judge my life and progress through external points of validation. I think about how much I weigh, how many paintings I sell as Kate the Artist, how many kids sign up for camp as Kate the Executive Director of Overnight Camps, how much money I fundraise as Kate the Nonprofit Leader, how many people interact with me on a social media post, etc.

I consider how productive I've been, how much I get done in a day, the feeling I get after interacting with a colleague, the feeling I get after interacting with a friend, the feeling I get after interacting with my mom, dad, sister or brother, the feeling I get after I interact with my children or my spouse.

Then I find myself getting a little deeper, a little closer to the mushy insides I've been trying to outsmart.

Oh....the feeling of being alone and interacting with myself.

On days when estrogen – The Big E, as I like to call it - is in the house, I'm pretty proud of my work, and have lots of energy to keep plugging away. Truthfully, I LOVE my work. I LOVE my environment, my family, my friends, my art. I've created a work of art that is my life, and more often than not, I recognize this.

However...

When I'm low on estrogen, it's HARD. I can be pretty darn hard on myself. On days that estrogen is low, I feel like a drugged slug. Like I don't do enough. Like everything is uphill and unfathomably difficult and I will never ever EVER get where I'm trying to go. When I'm back on The Big E upswing, this downward spiral strikes me as wild and hysterical and 100% fascinating, but while it's happening? Not so much.

I've been riding this fun and horrible and entertaining and vicious cycle of wins and worries, gratitude and gut-wrenching struggle for decades. Now, after months of studying a word that has been trying to teach me for years, I finally have a Truth to shout from the Mountain Top:

VALIDATION is an INSIDE JOB.

I'll repeat this, because it may be the most simple thing I've ever heard, and yet is so deep and complex we could spend our whole lives engaged in the study of it.

Validation is an inside job.

Initially when I began looking at the word I saw it as a need to be validated. And I do think that exists. It's a cry from deep inside - a quiet, vulnerable voice that's looking for approval, to be seen, to be heard, to be felt, to be needed, to be wanted, *to be enough.*

This voice wants to be part of a community. We are biologically wired for this yearning because we need others to survive and thrive. If we are accepted (for who we are) we can relax and let our greatest gifts shine. These greatest gifts are so unique. I can't tell you what they are. They're different for all of us. And guess what?

They're validated from the inside. (Big breath out. That is something!)

It may sound so simple, but I'm thinking this may be a deep one, like Brené Brown's work on Shame and Vulnerability. There is a powerful connection between VALIDATION, where we are the judge and juror of our own internal courtrooms, and fulfillment, the sweet contentment of living a life beyond our wildest dreams.

When we believe someone or something outside of ourselves is in charge of telling us our worth, we hand over the keys to our destiny.

So how, then, do we keep the keys for ourselves and hop into the driver's seat with joy, faith, and confidence?

Well, my friends, we must "LIVE ON PURPOSE."

This is one of my core life mantras and go-to phrases. It's 100% responsibility and 100% validation as an inside job. The call and commitment to LIVE ON PURPOSE can be incredibly powerful and totally scary at the same time. You see, if you are the one responsible for validation or validating yourself, there is no one to blame - *except yourself.*

So you must – you must! - create metrics that matter to you; metrics of validation tailored to your own true vision and virtues, so you know when you are on track for you.

What does this mean for you?

I'm so glad you asked.

VALIDATION: THE PERSONALIZED GAME PLAN

Let's look at a life where VALIDATION is an INSIDE JOB. Not surprisingly, the place to start is with an honest inventory of YOU – your goals, priorities, dreams, and desires. Use the space below to write down a few words or sentences for each category. These are your **BIG ROCKS**. I call these areas "Big Rocks" because of a very simple yet effective visual exercise helping us understand how important it is to protect our priorities, or lose them to life's merciless, time-stealing minions!

First, grab a jar or bucket, and fill it with Big Rocks. These represent your life's high-value ideals, goals, wish lists, concerns, and pursuits. (You'll be writing about these in the "Snapshot" section coming up.)

Next, add a bunch of smaller rocks — your next-level must-do's in life; obligations, responsibilities, and areas that need your time and attention in order to be a functional grownup in society, although they're not necessarily sexy, inspired, or soul-driven.

Now, add sand to your container. Watch as the sand fills in the spaces around the rocks. The sand represents all the things that come up during a regular day, week, month, or year; the stuff of life you don't necessarily write to-do lists about, but have to be handled or acknowledged nonetheless.

At this point, your container appears to be at capacity. Just like our lives, it doesn't look like you could possibly fit one more thing into the mix. There's no room, right?

Think again! Fill a cup of water and pour it into the container. This represents all the sneaky, unpredictable details that take our time and attention, drain our energy, and sometimes send us to the brink of batty if we weren't there already.

The moral of this exercise?

If we don't consciously put our Big Rocks in our container first, the Stuff of Life will quickly and effortlessly hijack their space, fill in the gaps, and make it extraordinarily difficult to include our Big Rocks in any viable or meaningful way. Conversely, if we add them first and understand their importance, everything else can fit around them.

So before you begin deciding upon and writing down your Big Rocks in the next section, take a few deep breaths, and invite your body to relax. Slowly, begin to tiptoe out of the hustle and bustle of your head and into the safe, sacred space of your heart.

Your head wants to tell you all the things you "should" write, "should" care about, "should" want.

Your heart will whisper the truth.

Your head will remember the opinions others have shared with you – a parent, a boss, a teacher, a friend – and shout them out as directives for your life.

Your heart will use compassion, grace, intuition, and love to reveal what matters to you.

On this journey toward truth, insights, and validation, let your heart lead the way.

THE QUICK AIRPLANE VIEW "BIG ROCKS" SNAPSHOT
FOR _____'S LIFE

Health and Wellness – Your Body

Family/Friends/Relationships – Your People

Career/Your Gift in the World – Your Work

Environment/Home/Day to Day – Your Soup

Spirit/Something Bigger Than Yourself – Your Connection

Finances/Feelings of Abundance – Your Freedom

Giving Back/Stewardship/Teaching/Philanthropy – Your Service

GETTING TO KNOW YOU ON ONE "PERFECT" DAY

What do you want in your daily life? Describe one simple, basic, perfect, regular day.

What are your some of your daily actions? What do you eat during this day? What fills you up? What makes you smile?

On the following page is a graph paper chart from something called a Bullet Journal. This is a tool I use to honor and document the Big Rocks of my life, and it's a strategy I think could help you, too.

I use the chart to quickly track and notice my daily habits, doing my best to align them with my life's priorities. Every day there are countless distractions and "bright, shiny objects" that can all too easily steal my time and attention. This tool is a way for me to distill hopes and goals into actionable steps that – ideally! – fuel my heart and soul.

In the left column, I simply write a few action steps from every major Big Rocks section in my life. These are not grand, sweeping acts of meaning and might, but thoughtful, realistic, and infinitely doable **micro actions** that serve as daily or weekly ambassadors for their categories. Then, at the end of the day or a few times a week, I look at my chart and mark the boxes if and when I've taken action.

That's it!

When you see the chart, hopefully it'll all make sense to you.

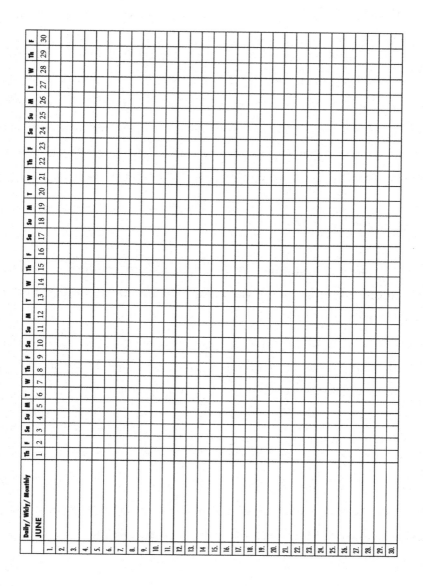

Why use the chart? Because the secret sauce of self-validation is found in our **DAILY HABITS**.

For example, I seem to always be on a "I want to lose weight" kick. You can replace this with any other goal - save more money, enjoy your spouse more, have more time to create, or simply enjoy what you have created, give more to others, share your gifts with more people, earn money from your passion, know what you are passionate about, feel more passion in your life, let your children go and grow, feel at peace…fill in the blank.

But then what? What do we do next?

If we take small, simple, <u>micro actions</u> toward progress in the area we want to improve, we are validating that we are committed to this idea.

Unfortunately, there's a dark side to validation. If we do not take action or even worse, do something that is in direct opposition to our desire, we are validating - putting into law, literally confirming to ourselves - that we do not truly want this change, this goal.

In my world, with every bite of something I know I should not eat, there is a confirming voice saying, "Tomorrow, we will do this tomorrow," validating that I really am not committed, that I am a failure.

WHY DO WE DO THIS?

Why do we validate in the opposite direction? In the negative?

The likely culprits are fear of change, fear of failure, fear of success, fear of the unknown...or sometimes it's just a sense of indifference, ambiguity, or uncertainty that nudges us to stray from our pristine path. The important thing is to realize that on both conscious and subconscious levels, we are validating ourselves through our actions, for better or for worse.

You've heard it said that "The TRUTH will set your free," right? Becoming aware of how deeply our daily actions are linked with our sense of validation is a vital step toward our sense of freedom.

What areas do you 100% validate in the direction of your goals and dreams?

What areas do you 75% validate, 50% validate, 25% validate?

But it's not always just about actions. We're not automatons. We're human, in all our messy, inexplicably human glory. How we FEEL is another amazing area where we validate or make law.

"I feel tired today." *"Really? You feel tired today? Have you written and committed to your list of daily practices that you know give you vitality? Have you validated the plan you already made? Or have you decided to wing it today?"*

More often than not, when I check in with myself, if I feel tired I probably didn't stick to the plan that inspires me, delights me, and aligns with my Big Rocks. Using my chart helps me see this, and (eventually) helps me make better decisions. I have surrendered to the fact that the Validation Game is a marathon, not a sprint, and while I'm not always perfect, **a little bit of steady progress over time makes a world of difference**.

You see, validation IS an inside job.

THE DO-BE-DO-BE-DO METHOD

There is a part of me that loves using the Do-Be-Do-Be-Do Method to life. I don't think it's smart to go 100% in without looking around and seeing if you are on course. Are you taking daily action in the right direction, or are you self sabotaging? If you're self sabotaging, you could ask yourself, "Why?" If you notice areas where you're progressing, see what's working and think about what you could do to enhance the other areas in which you wish to see progress.

Why is this so important? **I believe life satisfaction comes from consciously creating.** If you are called to be a healer or a knitter or a baker or an accountant…or a mom, a muse, a witness…then as you follow the call, the path or the way will be presented.

I am, with 100% of my being, striving to validate this idea. I actively choose to believe in hope and in personal accountability, and in giving and doing for those who can't do for themselves.

I choose to believe we can restore the health of our planet and create one world community that honors people, as well as the animals and oceans and land and air and the energy of all.

I choose to believe we can consciously evolve. To do this, we must play our parts. As hard as we can play. For as long as we are here on Earth.

We need to value the young and the old, the vital and the sick. We are the change. We are exactly what the world needs.

I am. WE are. YOU are.

YOU, at this age, at this height and weight, with your ideas, with your authentic power. Everything that has entered your world has been a gift. Everything.

Let's play with this, shall we?

You are not your feelings. You are not your emotions. You are the person who gets to validate them, and move them through you. You get to set your course and be the captain of your ship. You also have been given a magical gift of **intuition** and **connection** to something bigger than you - with a piece of it buried inside of you, like a radio tower or tuning fork - matching the world.

Your feelings, however, do serve as important guides, validating (or not!) if and when you are in harmony with the Universe.

Our job is to be conscious of what we emit and receive.

To **VALIDATE ON PURPOSE** but not in ignorance. This is the job for us – the scientists, the artists, the willing seekers and students of LIFE.

Life is precious.

We are so incredibly lucky to be here right now.

We are lucky to be alive – we've hit the lottery already. The odds that we are here right now, as an alive human, are 1 in 400 TRILLION.

Please do something with this.

Choose to validate in the direction of your dreams, live on purpose, create conscious communities, and leave this world a better place.

Thank you for playing.

If you ever want to bounce ideas off of me in an effort to move toward a life that validates your balanced, authentic self, please feel free to contact me at kate@katelemay.com or find me on Facebook, Instagram, YouTube, SnapChat, Twitter @katelemay, or at www.katelemay.com.

I also just published my first artist book with images and words dedicated to this idea. It has so much space for your notes, as I hope the ideas I have shared resonate with you and become your own.

I'm so grateful for your time and attention. Thank you for hearing and seeing me. I see you. I hear you. I know you are doing your work, and I am proud of you.

And when in doubt, please remember to say the following to yourself:

"I am enough."

"I have everything I need."

"I am so very grateful."

A QUICK LI'L DITTY

ABOUT THE CONTRIBUTOR

Kate Lemay

All ARTIST, part summer camp director.

Creator of the Free Time Project,

featuring more than 4,000 original,

chakra-inspired paintings.

Living on purpose,

creating conscious communities.

Learn more: **KateLemay.com**

Resonate [rez-uh-neyt]

verb (used without object), resonated, resonating.

1. to resound.

2. to act as a resonator; exhibit resonance.

3. *Electronics.* to reinforce oscillations because the natural frequency of the device is the same as the frequency of the source.

4. to amplify vocal sound by the sympathetic vibration of air in certain cavities and bony structures.

5. to produce a positive feeling, emotional response, or opinion:
an issue that clearly resonates with members of our community; a poem that resonates for me.

CHAPTER 3

RESONATE

BY JENNA PAIGE SARNO

The universe was created with one single sound, one single vibration.

We are all still connected to that vibration, and although our vibration may fluctuate, we will ultimately return back to that single vibration. I believe, personally, that in the many lives our souls have experienced, we carry the memory of the vibration when we connect to something or someone we love.

Our souls live in these bodies, and our souls are constantly searching for that special vibration that makes our souls sing.

To **resonate** is to be in harmony with frequency and vibration. We are aware when something is right for us in our guts, and we have all experienced this on a small – or large! – scale.

We are aware of this connection in our day-to-day lives, and on some level we are always searching for it. It could be something as simple as picking what you would like to eat for breakfast or choosing an outfit, or something as profound as looking at a person from across the room and knowing that you are both meant to be in each other's lives.

It is pure magic. It is connection. It is love.

RESONATE OR BUST!

I have been obnoxiously stubborn my entire life. Stubborn in the sense that if I do not resonate with something, if it does not make my soul fly and if it does not give me that funny tingly feeling in my heart, then I want absolutely nothing to do with it.

I was unaware there was a name for this until about five years ago. I realized I felt this deep connection of resonance at a young age and have been living my life trying to recreate that intense and passionate feeling.

When I was 14 years old, I experienced the magic of a live musician preforming from his heart. I was in awe, and it felt as if I had gone to another planet. I knew I wanted to play music in that moment. A few moments later, I had the pleasure of meeting this person. So, I began singing.

Flash forward five years when I picked up a guitar for the first time.

A week after I took my first lesson, that very same musician happened to be in town. As I was walking to his concert I walked right by him. We made eye contact, and my jaw must have dropped because he stopped at the edge of the corner and waited for me to come and talk to him. I told him **I resonated deeply** with the way he performed when I was 14 years old, and that it inspired me to play also. Then I shared how I was a brand new guitar player – I hadn't even written a song yet – and he said the next time we met, I would have a gold record.

Now, I don't know if that's true or not. Anything's possible! But the fact is, my life has unfolded in such a way that it has taken minimal effort for my music "career" to take off. **I connected and resonated with music at a young age and knew in my soul it was my "thing."** I have just simply played, written when I felt like it, played gigs when I felt like it, and quite honestly, the rest has sort of been handed to me. Opportunities keep showing up for me and it is beautiful. It gives me purpose and makes me know and feel that I'm doing exactly what I'm supposed to be doing.

Since then I have been consciously connecting with that feeling.

If a job, relationship, art form, et cetera, does not make my soul vibrate, I will not participate.

This may seem like a design flaw from the outside to some people, but to me it makes perfect sense.

You see, when we resonate with something – whether it's a person, place, creative outlet, job, idea, or opportunity – we know it's for us. We know it was written in the cosmos and ingrained in the story that's been laid out for us.

It's like connecting with an old friend.

Our souls get excited because in one way or another, we've been participating in whatever the act may be, for all of our souls' existence.

MY DREAM, YOUR MISSION

My dream for you is to find and connect, on a deep level, to that with which you resonate.

It doesn't require much work. It does, however, require you to be willing to clear the clutter of your mind, as well as all of the outside noise from society, family, and friends telling you what you're "supposed" to be doing.

The fastest, most foolproof way to make this powerful connection is to listen to your own heart. How will you know when you strike resonating gold? Time will stop, you'll become so engulfed with what you're experiencing that you'll be bathed in the bliss of the present moment, and you'll feel really, really, reeeeaaaalllly gooooooood.

I believe we should all focus more energy on the pursuit of spiritual, physical, and emotional resonance. When we allow our energy to get sidetracked and seduced by pursuits our souls don't absolutely LOVE, we're not only depleting and wasting our energy, we're dishonoring our gifts, moving further and further away from our joy, fulfillment, and life's purpose.

This also applies to our intuitive process of creativity.

34

When we allow ourselves to clear out life's non-resonating distractions, we begin to fall in line with our singular, spectacular TRUTH.

Herein lives the magic!

THE GIFT OF PROCRASTINATION

Let's take a moment to pay homage to an **unexpected ally** in the process of creative alignment and resonance, a force many of us are used to fighting, cursing, resenting, and even vilifying.

I'm talking about the simple yet glorious art of **procrastination.**

Procrastination leaves this beautiful space between the beginning of an idea and the end of the idea. This space invites the energy to flow, and the idea to grow into something bigger than it would have if we had forced or set restrictive deadlines for ourselves.

However, more often than not, we judge it – harshly, mercilessly! – as a failure in resourcefulness, a personality defect, or an unforgivable affront to time management.

Imagine planting a seedling in a pot of new soil. Then imagine getting angry and frustrated at the seedling because it refused to grow according to your desired deadline. Imagine losing respect for the seedling, losing faith in the seedling, and insisting the seedling was without talent, worth, beauty, or virtue. Then imagine giving up on it, grabbing it right out of the pot and throwing it to its demise, never to be tended to again.

Oh, the poor seedling! All it needed was some water, light, and love, and the proper amount of time to blossom! All it needed was for you to understand and appreciate the natural flow of its process, and it would have given you a beautiful flower.

What if we embraced procrastination as an essential part of our creative arsenal? What if we understood it as a brewing period; a time, place, and space for our unconscious to mull, dream, dismiss, discover, feel, connect, combust, explore, and invent our next work of art?

We must allow ourselves the time and space to line up with our truth, and allow the process to unfold naturally, safely, and without the ego's demagoguery. Rather than force our energy into activities that don't make our souls sing, **we can (and must!) choose to strengthen our muscles of self-compassion, grace, faith, patience, and perhaps most of all, LEVITY.**

We must get out of the way, take a breath, and let our seedlings blossom.

Now, imagine this as your new guiding Whisper of Wisdom:

There is no need to rush the process.

What will be, will be, all in perfect time. And when it's time to take action, you will know what to do and how to move forward from the inside out. You'll have the information and resources you need to succeed, and you will *feel* your way – instinctively, intuitively, exquisitely – to the next stage of your creative journey, whatever and wherever it may be.

TRUST YOUR TECHNOLOGY

Shine your light. Do what you LOVE.

You don't have to ask yourself if you love something – your heart will tell you on its own. **Your spiritual technology is designed to resonate with the frequencies of joy, ease, authenticity, and conscious evolution.**

Procrastinate enough to understand what makes your soul sing, what resonates with YOU. Then give yourself the ROOM to BLOOM, to create and to express with lightness and love, and without expectations.

You might be surprised at what you create.

A QUICK LI'L DITTY

ABOUT THE CONTRIBUTOR

Jenna Paige Sarno

Yoga teaching,

music making,

health coaching traveler.

Empowering women to live

their most authentic lives.

Creator, "You, Without the Mask" movement.

Learn more: **Facebook.com/JennaSarnoMusic**

Communicate [kuh-myoo-ni-keyt]

verb (used with object), communicated, communicating.

1. to impart knowledge of; make known:
to communicate information; to communicate one's happiness.
2. to give to another; impart; transmit:
to communicate a disease.
3. to administer the Eucharist to.
4. Archaic. to share in or partake of.

verb (used without object), communicated, communicating.

5. to give or interchange thoughts, feelings, information, or the like, by writing, speaking, etc.:
They communicate with each other every day.
6. to express thoughts, feelings, or information easily or effectively.
7. to be joined or connected:
The rooms communicated by means of a hallway.
8. to partake of the Eucharist.
9. *Obsolete.* to take part or participate.

CHAPTER 4

COMMUNICATE

BY CHRISTINA ALEXA

Clear communication is an art and a gift. Mastering the practice of communication requires patience, neutrality, and the willingness to embrace vulnerability. This practice leads us through the layers of who we are *not*, directly to the truth of our authentic nature. Along the way we must face levels of denial, fear, and core beliefs that represent misinterpretations of who we think we are.

Clear communication requires that **our warrior self must be activated**, armored and ready for action to slay the inner adversary that strives to protect the ego and deflect the truth. If we are accustomed to clinging to our comfort zone in order to avoid the risk of perceiving our own needs and using our voice, then we also have likely experienced the inevitable truth that **our authentic nature will always shine through**, regardless of the steadfast obligation to our defenses.

What we resist persists. Whether we are the willing hero/heroine or the *unwilling* hero/heroine, we will all eventually arrive in the seat of purity because our spirit demands it.

This is good news.

DISCOVERING OUR AUTHENTIC NATURE

The pathway to our authentic nature can be fraught with resistance to feeling, seeing, and acknowledging parts of ourselves because we are afraid to feel shame and self-blame; we are afraid of change. We know that our lives might change if we commit to honesty and truth. We spend so much time preserving and fortifying our comfort zone that we forget how to take risks.

Yet healthy risk is the wind beneath our wings, the refreshing breath that exhilarates our soul. Committing to truth is inherently risky, but only if we are afraid of the change that brings healthy alignment. Fear is expected and allowed for; we can shake in our boots and move forward anyway. **To become a clear communicator we must have the willingness to commit to ourselves, to the truth of who we are.** The truth of who we are is our authentic self. We must have the spark, the desire for freedom, for liberation of our authentic self.

COMMITTING TO TRUTH

The first step to clear communication is to commit to your own **truth.**

What does that mean?

Committing to truth is like committing to a **sacred marriage**. When we commit to a marriage with a partner we say that we will be there through thick or thin, we will embrace the highs and lows equally. We know that marriage is not always going to be easy, but the reward of love and companionship assists us through the tough times.

Sometimes when we commit we might not know what we are getting ourselves into, but **we are driven by the natural desire to love and be loved**. Without quite realizing we are doing it, we intuitively trust the process.

When we commit to our truth, **we are committing to our own divinity**, to the sacred marriage of self with higher self.

Just as in a marriage with a spouse, we can't foresee all of the ebbs and flows, the challenges and joys to come. We move forward with the faith that originates from the bedrock of our authentic nature.

HONORING THE SACRED MARRIAGE

Sacred marriage is a big step, one that brings permanent life change.

Why does marriage scare us? Perhaps because we know that **once we commit, we must stay present and accountable**. Marriage between self and our own divine nature is powerful, prone to the forces of our energetic nature, and intertwined with the broader forces of creation. Marriage with our divine self is an important step that precedes marriage with another.

However, our lives might not unfold that way.

We might fall in love and enter relationship with another long before we become aware of the importance of divine commitment with self. The good news is, there is no statute of limitations on coming into conscious relationship with ourselves.

Relationships offer a challenging way to grow spiritually, yet even in the absence of romantic relationship we can become absolutely fulfilled in sacred relationship with our divine nature. **When we are committed to ourselves, we grow because we are accountable and responsible.** We are committed to our own truth and sense of self. When we value ourselves, we have the capacity to hold others in a place of value, compassion, and even love.

LISTENING

The second step to clear communication is to develop the ability to **listen**.

If we can listen to ourselves, then we can listen to others. There are many ways to perceive what our authentic nature is trying to communicate. Our authentic nature wants to be self-aware and realized. Our ego nature also wants to thrive. Thus, the fodder from which war is born.

If we can face the internal war between our true nature and who we are *not* - and learn to suffer with grace the one hundred thousand deaths of the ego (easier said than done!) - we will have found the pathway to peace.

Above all else, this is a worthy effort because it will **radiate** out to all other meaningful aspects of our lives.

When we can listen to ourselves clearly, we are communicating. When we acknowledge our truth, we know we are communicating clearly with ourselves.

While at times it may be painful, the pain is only the death of self-image and of the ego. **Once we have the ability to communicate clearly with ourselves, all of the relationships around us become brighter, better, deeper, more authentic.**

When we embrace the most authentic version of ourselves, we become fulfilled.

APPRECIATING THE MIRROR

Clear communication provides a **mirror**.

Without the mirror of ourselves through others we might not hold ourselves accountable. We might not see as clearly our blind spots, or how it is we operate.

Without the mirror we also might not see our gifts as clearly, or know how it is that we impact others.

Without the mirror, we may stay trapped in patterns of behavior longer than we need to, patterns of suffering that lead us further away from **liberation**, the joy and light of pure freedom.

LETTING GO

Part of the risk of communicating rests in our fear of how we are perceived.

Whether we are afraid of hurting others, fear judgment, or if we feel the need to care take the emotions of others, communicating can feel risky. **Communication requires great courage and self-validation, as well as the ability to let go of the outcome.**

We cannot be attached to the result of our communications. Rather, prior to a communication we must take ownership and responsibility for our feelings; we must come to peace, or we will communicate with a "charge." IF we communicate with an emotional charge, we will invite a reaction every time.

An emotional charge is indicative of a lack of peace, ownership, and responsibility. It's an indication we are not yet fully "cooked" enough to make a clear communication.

PEACE

Peace is not found in emotion or thought.

The generous, consistent explosion of the senses through feeling and touch, through seeing and hearing, is not where peace is found. **Even in truth, peace distinguishes itself as a companion, not as native austerity.**

Peace is a vast and constant space that permeates all motions of consciousness, a subtle observance that once found becomes as loud and obvious as the Earth itself, the expansive and ever-present sky. Even on our best days we can forget to notice the clouds, the sunrise or the sunset, taking for granted they will always be there day after day. When we are ready we will notice, but not now. We are too busy.

Peace is like the very air we breathe; enveloping and penetrating, and often over looked.

The peace of living in our truth with the ability to self-advocate, whether when facing our own ego or others, is sublime. We have all heard the expression, "speak truth to power." This expression can be applied to ourselves as easily as to others.

When we give our power away, the cycle of projection > blame > resentment begins. We resent those we give our power to instead of taking personal responsibility. **Responsibility is freedom.** Who do we give our power to most often? The ego?

In **self-validating** we no longer need to give our power away, and peace becomes our truth.

THE 8 STEPS FOR TRUTH, PEACE, AND CLEAR COMMUNICATION

1. **"Ahimsa" / non-harming:** Release judgmental inner dialogue.

2. **Observe!** Witness your feelings from a place of neutrality, non-judgment.

3. **Honesty:** Have the courage to feel your own truth.

4. **Feel:** Experience the purity of feeling without the need to suppress, express, react, or distract. Just FEEL.

5. **Validate:** Honor what you observe and take ownership.

6. **Take responsibility:** When we own what we feel there is no need to blame or shame self or others.

7. **Value:** Recognize you deserve to own this truth, to experience fulfillment.

8. **Voice:** When we can't let go, communicate.

A QUICK LI'L DITTY

ABOUT THE CONTRIBUTOR

Christina Alexa

Keeper of the Lodge,
intuitive healer,
yoga teacher,
Reiki Master in the Usui tradition,
professional woodworker.
Owner and lead trainer,
The Abhyasa Yoga Institute.

Learn more: **ChristinaAlexa.com**

Appreciate [uh-pree-shee-eyt]

verb (used with object), appreciated, appreciating.

1. to be grateful or thankful for:
They appreciated his thoughtfulness.
2. to value or regard highly; place a high estimate on:
to appreciate good wine.
3. to be fully conscious of; be aware of; detect:
to appreciate the dangers of a situation.
4. to raise in value.

verb (used without object), appreciated, appreciating.

5. to increase in value:
Property values appreciated yearly.

CHAPTER 5

APPRECIATE

BY ALLEN VOIVOD

Gratitude.

I can't tell you how many times over the years the concept of gratitude has been recommended to me.

As a means to increase the level of satisfaction with my life, when the circumstances of my life were anything but satisfying.

As a means to welcome more abundance in my life, even though I could never shake the feeling certain things were lacking in my life.

As a means to bolster the happiness of those around me, even though I felt I was doing more for their happiness than they were doing for mine. Not their fault. Not that I could or would let them make me happy in the first place. I'd have to feel I deserved it for that to even be possible.

I'd like to tell you I'm at the point where I've solved these challenges. I'd like to tell you it was easier than I ever expected it would be.

I haven't. It's not.

The truth, I suspect, is that I continue to make it harder for myself, that I sabotage myself, that I take two steps back for each one I take forward. As John Popper of the band Blues Traveler once sang about life, *"It's that game that we play and we play it well/In fact we're so damn good that we try to lose."*

Then, take into consideration that I have a wife, business partner, friend, confidant, and supporter who deeply understands the value, the power, and the simple rightness of gratitude. Who has shared this with me in as many ways as she can devise to communicate. And she's devised quite a lot of them. If anyone has a shot of successfully grasping the concept of gratitude, it should be me.

Yet I resist.

I fight it. I want things to be the way I want them to be, and I want the Universe to meet me on my terms. I convince myself that I've gone more, more, so much more than halfway, and it's high time the Universe got off its duff and did me the courtesy of going that little bit of the rest of the way.

Try as I might, I learned that I can't get to gratitude without a bridge.

These days, the bridge isn't as necessary as it once was. But there are still days – more than I'd like to admit – where I can't make it to gratitude without some other ingredient to help make it happen. No, I'm not talking about coffee, or drugs, or therapy, or even aromatherapy.

What I can tell you for certain is this:

Appreciation has been the best bridge I've ever built for getting to the fertile and fruitful land of gratitude.

UNDERSTANDING THE APPRECIATION GAP

For me, the first level of appreciation was academic.

I may not have been able to feel that holy grail of gratitude, but I was raised well enough to be polite. I could understand when people had done things for me – my family, my circumstances – that deserved a measure of thanks. It's not like I was stingy with my gratefulness. I made sure people knew I appreciated their efforts.

But for me, the act of expressing gratefulness was more of an "act." It was more about managing what people thought about me as a person.

When people talk about caring what other people think of them, there are multiple levels. I put cat memes and Star Wars graphics in work presentations. I've been known to dance on barstools, take my shirt off in restaurants, wear wigs on any occasion, and otherwise do things that would make others feel self-conscious. In that sense, I don't often care what other people think about me.

On the other hand, I don't ever want people to think I'm ungrateful. I want people to have a good impression of me. So when someone does something nice, I do the right thing and demonstrate the appreciation the person deserves. External stimulus, external response.

Don't get me wrong - the appreciation I show is genuine. Just because I don't tingle with goose bumps when I say "Thank you" to someone, that doesn't mean I'm any less sincere or authentic about it. But once the societal transaction is over, it's not like I sit there suffused with gratitude afterward. It just vanishes. The gesture is real, but the emotional charge doesn't change.

It's my issue, not theirs, that sometimes my appreciation stops at my neck, so to speak.

It's mental. It's logical. It's rational. It's not always *feeling*, not always felt emotionally. Not because of anything done or not done by the other person. It's not them, it's me.

The good news is, committing the socially approved "act of appreciation" is part of building the bridge to the Holy Land of Authentic Gratitude. But if I settled for just acting the part of the Grateful Fellow Human Being, the benefits of true gratitude would forever be out of my reach.

I had to uplevel my appreciation game. I had to go from the external to the internal.

PRACTICE MAKES PRACTICE

My wife Lani talks about practice in the context of a few different things, yoga chief among them. No, yoga hasn't been an answer for me – again, more because I haven't allowed it to be. But the idea of a "practice" in general is an accessible one to me.

For me, getting to gratitude through appreciation requires practice – the practice of generating appreciation from within.

I realized I had to implement a practice of appreciation when the societal transaction wasn't there. And because I had been resistant to the idea of a regular gratitude-like practice, I needed to find a way to sneak appreciation into my system, when I would be vulnerable enough to allow myself to feel it. Kind of like stuffing a fistful of spinach into a yummy chocolate and peanut butter smoothie. My goal was to get the benefits without the Gratitude Gravitas.

The answer, for me, was to begin my appreciation practice as I dropped off to sleep.

BUT FIRST, A HELPFUL LITTLE STORY ABOUT PANIC

Before I explain the brilliant appreciation sneak attack that slipped past the defenses of my uncooperative ego, it's worth mentioning this: In the summer of 2001, I started having something akin to panic attacks at night.

The first night it happened, I got in bed, lights out, and expected the usual – to fall off into dreamland. Instead, lying in the dark, I suddenly started freaking out. I was afraid I was going to die in my sleep, and I have long been DEEPLY afraid of dying. Frantic heartbeat night after night, short and rapid breathing, awful chills coursing through my body, yet I was sweating like a madman at the same time.

No, there was nothing wrong in my life. I'd been married nearly a year, no kids on the way yet, money was fine, health was fine, families were fine. No explanation for it. Just crazy all-of-a-sudden panic. I was unaccountably, outrageously super-afraid of sleep. And closing my eyes made it worse.

To calm myself, to stop the tornado of terrible thoughts and get some halfway-decent rest, I resorted to a tactic I'd used when I was a kid and had trouble shutting down at night.

Think about your clothes right now. They've likely been on you for a while, so you can't exactly "feel" them, because your nerve endings have stopped sending you signals about them.

Well, as a kid lying in bed, after a while I couldn't "feel" the bed. So I imagined myself getting lighter and lighter, and floating up from the bed – because I couldn't feel the bed, so I might as well be floating, right? First my head, then my torso, all the way down to my feet and ankles. By the time I got down that far, I was usually already asleep.

This technique returned to help me again when I was having my nightly mini-panic bedtime episodes in my early thirties. So when it came to the practice of feeling appreciation in my early forties – with kids, a house, a business, and a hustling and bustling life – embedding the appreciation in that floating feeling seemed to be the most natural, muscle-memoried thing to do.

Next, I did what Lani suggested in trying to think of different things to appreciate each night. The rule she had suggested was that I wasn't supposed to appreciate the same people or the same things over and over, that I was supposed to build the muscle by always finding new people for whom to be thankful. **But as Tony Robbins says, "Complexity is the enemy of execution."**

So a lot of times, Lani and the kids were on the list every night. Different things about them each day, at least.

I would let myself sink into the bed, wait to stop "feeling" the bed, then imagine myself floating, and begin the list. Lani's smile. One son's half-asleep hug in the morning. Another son reaching to hold my hand even though by all rights he's old enough to be "too cool" to do that. Little things. Sometimes bigger things, too, but most often, little things.

And 99 times out of 100, the little things were enough.

BETTER LIVING THROUGH SCIENCE

Thanks to a series of "moral dilemma" experiments, the cognitive psychologist Lawrence Kohlberg delineated a set of stages in one's moral development. At the lower end is **pre-conventional morality**, whereby one's behavior is driven by either **getting rewards or avoiding punishment**.

The second level is **conventional morality**, where **external approval** and the rules and laws of society drive one's behavior.

The third and final level is **post-conventional morality**, where rules and laws can be seen as unjust, and where **moral principles** like equality, justice, and so forth become more important, guiding one's behavior like an internal compass.

What I had been doing by default – giving appreciation as a matter of reputation and correctness – was at that second level, of conventional morality. **This, Kohlberg argued, is where most people get stuck.** In his observations, most people in society don't progress from conventional to post-conventional morality.

And that's exactly what was happening with me. I was stuck. Emotionally, mentally, circumstantially.

When I took the next step, **when I added the practice of appreciation as a nighttime ritual, things began to change for me.**

Here's what I notice when I do it on a regular basis. It doesn't happen overnight (pun intended), but the more regularly I'm able to do it, the more often the following things happen.

- I wake up in a **better mood**.

- The better mood **lasts longer**.

- **It's easier** for me – an introvert by nature – to get along with people.

- I'm **more patient** with my kids.

- I'm **more able to look for solutions and workarounds** to issues than sink into frustration and resignation.

- I'm **kinder to myself**. Negative self-talk, though it doesn't entirely go away, can occasionally recede quietly into the darkness of whatever evil place from which it arises.

- Rather than just going through the motions of life, **I actually enjoy life** in its imperfect glory. (Heck, I can occasionally even laugh at myself!)

From the big-picture standpoint, I'm able to step outside of myself and see how lucky I and my family really are and continue to be, even when life seems like a chaotic mess.

That's how I was finally able to feel the appreciation. **Feeling it feels good.** It feels right. It becomes part of a virtuous circle that makes everything feel better.

THE SECRET OF APPRECIATION

Yes, Lani recommended the **attitude of gratitude** to me. She was the first and foremost. Yes, all the gurus tell you to do it, too. So you could be forgiven for thinking that my finally getting with the program was still in that second level of morality.

But when I started, I didn't tell anyone – not even Lani – that I had actually started a secret practice of appreciation. For me, keeping the practice quiet was the key to getting to the next level of morality, and finally getting to some tangible results, instead of continuing to stomp my foot and wait for the Universe to make a move.

What my practice does, I think, is to open a connection with the Universe that I'd previously been unable to make.

By keeping my practice secret, I wasn't looking for anyone's approval, and there was no law that could tell me to do it or not do it. By being private, my devotion to the practice of appreciation was pure, and keeping it pure made it easier to accept and practice the idea of embedding the **vibration of appreciation** into my very skin.

Keeping an act like this secret was a thing I'd picked up as a kid, too, thanks to my Bible school upbringing. From Matthew 6:5-6:

And when you pray, do not be like the hypocrites. For they love to pray standing in the synagogues and on the street corners to be seen by men ... But when you pray, go into your inner room, shut your door, and pray to your Father, who is unseen. And your Father, who sees what is done in secret, will reward you.

MY MIDNIGHT CONFESSIONS

Yes, I'm now revealing the appreciation practice I've kept secret, by writing this for you. There's a little tickle in the back of my brain you could call superstitious, which wonders whether the "magic" of appreciation will still work for me by telling you what I've been doing in the middle of the night.

I'm so honored and flattered to have been asked to contribute to this book for you, however, that I feel like the best thing I can do is tell you the truth of what happened for me.

To continue being truthful: I'm not consistent with it. Even when I am, it doesn't exactly make me an enlightened master or anything like that.

When I engage the feeling of appreciation, though, when consciously I weave that vibration into the physical *feeling* of my body, I feel better. I am better. And the world is better around me.

I hope reading this can make things better for you, too.

A QUICK LI'L DITTY
ABOUT THE CONTRIBUTOR

Allen Voivod

Dad, biz storyteller,

social media Jedi:

Epiphanies, Inc.

Ally in Possibility,

speaker, leader:

"A-Ha!" Tribe.

World's only daily

Star Wars podcaster:

Star Wars 7x7.

Learn more: **AllenVoivod.com**

Liberate [lib-uh-reyt]

verb (used with object), liberated, liberating.

1. to set free, as from imprisonment or bondage.

2. to free (a nation or area) from control by a foreign or oppressive government.

3. to free (a group or individual) from social or economic constraints or discrimination, especially arising from traditional role expectations or bias.

4. to disengage; set free from combination, as a gas.

5. *Slang.* to steal or take over illegally:

The soldiers liberated a consignment of cigarettes.

CHAPTER 6

LIBERATE

BY KELLY LANG

How far off is your **freedom**?

Do you imagine a time when you will **feel more free** in your life?

Maybe it's when you finish school or the big project, or when you can finally start your own business, or when your kids are out of diapers or go off to college. Or, maybe you'll *finally feel free* when you retire. Perhaps it's when you've acquired enough financial wealth to travel, or work less, or do things you've long desired to do.

We all have our own definition of freedom and how long it will be before we arrive at that destination. Do you measure your path to freedom in days, weeks, months, or years?

What if freedom was only minutes away, and you could get there without changing anything tangible in your life?

If you have five minutes to ask yourself the following questions, you may find that **freedom is not that far off at all**.

#1: WHO'S THE BOSS?

Whether you work for someone else or yourself, or don't work at all, recognize **every single thing you do is a choice**, including your own thoughts.

If you work too much - that is your choice. You might argue, "No, I have to work this much to pay my bills!" However, you *do* have the choice to *not* pay your bills, so simply recognize you do in fact have a choice.

If you have anything that feels like it prevents you from being free, ask yourself: "Who is making me do this? Who's the boss here?" Once you realize that you are 100% responsible for your choices, you can let go of blaming other people or circumstances or the general unfairness of life.

Everything is a choice, and **once you accept that you are the boss, you will feel more free**.

#2: WHAT IS MY SOUL HUNGRY FOR?

It's easy to go through life without checking in with what your soul needs most. But simply asking this question, checking in with yourself and **listening**, can give you a sense of freedom. Do this right now and see what you hear.

Maybe the answer is fresh air or stillness. Or perhaps it's singing, laughter, or connection. It could be one of a million different things because we are all different. In many cases, **it can take just a moment to acknowledge and feed your soul.**

Granted, once you hear the answer, you can takes steps to give yourself the freedom to have more of what your soul is hungry for in your life. But even in the moment you ask the question, **sometimes just a breath of fresh air, a 12-second hug, or a minute of laughter can release you** from the feeling of being stifled, unfulfilled, or simply un-free.

#3. WHAT FREEDOM DO I ALREADY HAVE?

Recognize and count all the freedoms you already have.

If you can walk, you have more freedom than many people. Think about newborns or the elderly, as well as those with injuries, illness, or disabilities.

Celebrate that you have the freedom to read the books you choose or worship as you please or wear the clothing you prefer. These may seem simple but we often forget to acknowledge and appreciate all the freedoms we already have.

Even if you cannot come up with a long list of freedoms, remember this: **You always have freedom in your mind.** No one else can control your thoughts.

This was the secret strategy that Nazi concentration camp survivor

Viktor Frankl employed to survive. Despite his imprisonment, harsh treatment, and witnessing the worst of atrocities, Viktor Frankl kept his mind positive by envisioning a completely different world. The Nazis may have had control over his body, but they never gained control of his mind.

So even in times when you may feel you're lacking freedom, celebrate the freedom that already (and always!) exists within you.

#4. WHO CAN I FORGIVE TODAY?

Forgiveness is one of the golden keys to freedom.

When you hold onto resentment or blame, you are holding yourself in the negativity of whatever experience caused the original hurt. You are allowing the past to keep you in a pattern that prevents you from feeling free or moving fully forward.

Forgiving doesn't mean condoning the wrong that was done to you, but it is the only way to release your attachment, as well as the impact of the negativity on your life.

When you resist forgiveness, continuing to blame another, you're putting yourself in the victim hot tub. It may feel good for a time, but if you stay there too long, life will pass you by.

#5. WHAT DOES MY VISION OF FREEDOM LOOK LIKE?

It might be a clear picture of being on a beach in the Caribbean, or on a big boat in the Atlantic, or travelling through Europe. It actually doesn't matter what it is. **What matters is how you feel when you envision it.**

That *feeling* is what you really equate with freedom, and you can have that feeling just by **allowing yourself** to be fully present in that vision.

See yourself enjoying the warmth, or the sun, or whatever **your vision of freedom** holds, and imagine it like a movie playing in your mind.

When you notice you are smiling, you will undoubtedly feel more free.

#6. IS THERE ONE THING ON MY TO-DO LIST THAT I CAN GIVE MYSELF PERMISSION NOT TO DO (TODAY)?

This might be hard at first – especially if productivity is your #1 measure of a good day – but give it a shot.

Is there one thing that you can let go of for today, one chunk of time that you can **free up for yourself**, even if it's just five minutes?

Ask yourself, "Do I *really* have to do that today?"

In most cases, you'll find there are truly only a few things on your list that really have to get done on that day. Most of the other tasks can wait a day or two or even longer. I'm not suggesting you become a perpetual procrastinator. However, every now and then, especially when you feel most concerned about getting everything done, do this exercise and let go ... just a little.

When you **give yourself permission to say NO** to something you self-imposed upon yourself, you're not only offering yourself a beautiful kindness, you're reminding yourself **you are the boss**, and **you can choose freedom** through conscious and compassionate decision-making.

#7. WHAT TRUTH AM I HOLDING ONTO?

When we hold our own truth inside of ourselves instead of showing it or speaking it, we can feel imprisoned.

Speaking your mind and sharing your views, or just living your life authentically, is an incredibly freeing experience. If you don't normally do this – if instead you keep it all in, hiding yourself and your true thoughts and feelings – you might need to practice with little things first.

Tell the truth the next time someone upsets you. **Learn the art of communicating your truth** without getting charged up about it, so you can share your thoughts and views in a way that is constructive vs. argumentative.

Embrace the reality that while you cannot predict or control a person's response to what you have to say, you *can* choose to disengage from any automatic reactions born in defensiveness, resentfulness, anger, fear, blame, or ego-tainted unkindness.

As you become more seasoned at speaking your truth without attachment to the response, you'll gain more confidence, clarity, and a growing sense of alignment with your dreams and potential.

FEELING, FUELING, AND BEING YOUR FREEDOM

As you have hopefully realized through the process of answering these seven powerful questions, the path to your freedom relies on your faith, capacity for self awareness, and commitment to self love.

You must believe in the core of your being you deserve to be happy, you deserve to feel free.

Shifting your mindset from victimhood to liberation is a journey of empowerment, creativity, forgiveness, and gentle yet vigilant grace. Honor your vision. Stay the course. Nourish yourself with the ideas, ideals, activities, and communities that help you feel and celebrate your freedom.

You deserve to be happy. You deserve to feel free.

FREEDOM FOCUS

1. How much freedom do you feel you have in your life right now? Please use a scale of 1-10, where 10 is absolute freedom and 1 is the complete absence of freedom. _____

2. Why is that number not lower?

3. In what areas of your life would you like to experience more freedom? (e.g. career, relationships, creative pursuits, finances, physical body/movement/clothing choices)

4. What would it look like if you had more freedom?

5. Who do you need to get permission from to create the freedom you desire?

6. When will that happen?

7. What is holding you back or preventing you from creating more freedom?

8. What competing beliefs or commitments are in the way?

9. If you could wave a magic wand and be free of any one thing right now, what would you choose?

10. Can you picture life with that freedom already established?

11. Are you smiling?

A QUICK LI'L DITTY

ABOUT THE CONTRIBUTOR

Kelly Lang

Mom, yoga instructor,
certified nutrition counselor,
freedom coach.
Young Living Essential Oils
distributor, team leader,
educator, enthusiast.
Author of
Live Free and Dream:
7 Steps to Manifest
Your True Life Desires.

Learn more: **LiveFreeKelly.com**

Concentrate [kon-suhn-treyt]

verb (used with object), concentrated, concentrating.

1. to bring or draw to a common center or point of union; converge; direct toward one point; focus:
to concentrate one's attention on a problem; to concentrate the rays of the sun with a lens.
2. to put or bring into a single place, group, etc.:
The nation's wealth had been concentrated in a few families.
3. to intensify; make denser, stronger, or purer, especially by the removal or reduction of liquid:
to concentrate fruit juice; to concentrate a sauce by boiling it down.
4. *Mining.* to separate (metal or ore) from rock, sand, etc., so as to improve the quality of the valuable portion.

verb (used without object), concentrated, concentrating.

5. to bring all efforts, faculties, activities, etc., to bear on one thing or activity (often followed by on or upon):
to concentrate on solving a problem.
6. to come to or toward a common center; converge; collect:
The population concentrated in one part of the city.
7. to become more intense, stronger, or purer.

CHAPTER 7

CONCENTRATE

BY RODERICK RUSSELL

If you were able to ask childhood me what I wanted to be when I grew up, the answer would not surprise you.

Like many young boys, I had dreams of being an astronaut. I loved math and science, but more than that I loved the stars and exploration. Becoming an astronaut was the perfect blend of those elements.

As I grew I became more practical. Realizing my slim odds of going into space (though odds are rising now that we're on the verge of commercial civilian space travel!), I became more focused on astronomy and astrophysics.

Physics and my continued desire to explore led me toward nuclear propulsion engineering. If I couldn't go up into space, let's go down in submarines! Reasonably, I have zero interest in being confined in a tin can — either high up in the sky or deep down in the ocean — but my interest in "going where no one has gone before" was so intense that I was willing to put up with the discomfort.

Physics, astronomy, and math gave way to neuroscience, which led me into computer science. Computer science niched itself down into artificial intelligence research. Suddenly, I was eager to spend my life in a laboratory trying to build an artificial brain.

But that interest too evolved once I realized that it wasn't computer science, nor cognitive science, computational neuroscience or any of the "sciences" that I was fundamentally interested in.

Instead, what had been fueling my exploration was a deep-seated need to understand who we are. You and me, as humans. And throughout my early years it was simply manifesting in multifarious ways. All varied attempts to understand our place in the universe, how – and why – we work the way we do.

So naturally, realizing my pull toward the "big questions," I focused my studies on philosophy. That most useful of college majors. You've heard the joke: What's the difference between a philosophy degree and a bench? A bench can support a family.

I've had lots of dreams. Lots of interests. I've studied many things throughout my life and have had several careers. But never, not once, and not in a million years did this career appear on my "what I want to be when I grow up" list:

Professional Sword Swallower

Yet here I am. Deeply entrenched in what has been the longest career of my life, stretching almost two decades now, as a professional sword swallower.

As unexpected as the career choice has been, it is, in many ways, the most natural progression. Swallowing swords was quite literally the next logical thing. Trust me, I studied formal logic.

I now spend my life traveling the country performing and speaking to audiences of all stripes. Sometimes I aim strictly to entertain. Other times it's my duty to educate.

But behind it all are two consistent goals: Connect and Communicate.

CONNECTING AND COMMUNICATING

I build a very specific message into my stage presentations. One that I hope impacts my audiences deeply. But as with much in life, most of the real work happens behind the scenes. After the show. When the fourth wall of the stage is down, and I get to speak directly and personally with people.

The most common question I get is this: How do you swallow swords? The answer to which is pretty dry.

I dutifully explain the anatomy of it all, the physiological obstacles, and the mental skills I employ. The things that can and occasionally do go wrong. But really it comes down to this: What you see is what you get.

There's no grand trick or technique.

The question that really gets me going though, the one that is asked far less often but offers the most profound opportunity to connect and communicate is this: *Why* do I swallow swords?

I'll be the first to tell you that swallowing swords is not fun. Not even Type II Fun (fun in retrospect). It's not comfortable or pleasant in any way. And I don't get any particular rush or excitement from it.

What I do get is this: Focus.

If I'm called on for a sound bite response to the question of why I swallow swords, it comes out something like this: "**I'm interested in exploring the limits of human experience and ability**, and swallowing swords allows me to explore my own personal limits."

I fear there's so much secretly packed into that statement, however, that it fails to truly communicate the scope of what I mean.

Let me attempt to do it justice here.

THE MOST IMPORTANT GOAL OF LIFE

Have you ever been so lost in an activity, so **fully engaged**, that time seems to distort? Five minutes seeming like five hours or, more often, five hours seeming like five minutes?

So **in-the-moment** that your sense of self seems to drop away? You forget who you are and where you are and the only thing that exists is the present moment?

Have you ever been so absorbed that you forget to even think about your next action, because **it flows effortlessly** from the last?

This experience of selflessness, timelessness, effortlessness and well-being goes by many names. Athletes call it being **"in the zone"** while musicians call it being **"in the pocket."** It's a state of being well-known to Eastern spiritual practices – including all forms of Buddhism, Hinduism and yogic traditions – each of which have their own name for it.

In the West it has been spoken of by many of the psychology greats, including Abraham Maslow, who defined **the idea of peak experiences as being the "rare, exciting, oceanic, deeply moving, exhilarating, elevating experiences that generate an advanced form of perceiving reality**, and are even mystic and magical in their effect upon the experimenter."[1]

Maslow went so far as to consider "peak experience to be one of the most important goals of life, as it is **an indication of self-actualization**."[2]

More recently, the work of Hungarian psychologist Mihály Csíkszentmihályi has given us the technical term **Flow**[3] to describe these states of non-ordinary consciousness, where we exist in **a frictionless, effortless state of optimal performance**.

These states all exist on a continuum, some being more profound than others, but all sharing similar characteristics. And to some extent, most of us have experienced these moments, even if fleetingly.

A profound side effect of achieving these states is that we work in ways that blow the doors off our normally perceived limits.

A ten year study conducted by the McKinsey & Company consultancy group has shown that executives in flow are **500 percent more productive** than their counterparts.[4]

A research study at the University of Sydney reveals **creativity increases eightfold** as a result of flow.[5]

And it's been shown that while in flow, time to learn a new task can be cut in half, and in some studies, **learning has been accelerated a full ten times**.[6]

Imagine learning a new language in six weeks instead of six months!

This **is the power of flow.**

Yet more important than the measurable results of flow - undoubtedly a topic of interest to the productivity-oriented Western mindset – flow (and related experiences on the peak experience continuum) drastically increases our well-being, happiness, and life satisfaction. Not only does it make us better at everything, it fulfills us more than any other pursuit.

It is *autotelic* – an end in itself – having within itself the very purpose of its existence.

SO WHAT DOES ALL THIS HAVE TO DO WITH SWALLOWING SWORDS?

Here's the thing about flow and peak experiences – they don't happen randomly. They are the result of very specific triggers. Triggers both internal and external.

The doorway to each of these states on the continuum is the same. Over the years, psychological research has become more adept at uncovering exactly what these triggers are, and how exactly we can pull them to help reach these transcendent states.

Can you guess what the **one consistent, most powerful trigger** to these states happens to be?

If you guessed focus, you'd be right. **Flow follows <u>focus</u>.**

Primary to the flow experience is **concentration**, focus, one-pointed attention.

You see this trigger present in all of the most popular methods of achieving flow, from extreme sports to meditation, yoga, or playing an instrument. Surgeons report finding flow while operating, and you better believe that they are concentrating. Even something as simple as reading a book or walking can induce flow – as long as it's primed with *focus*.

As it turns out, extreme athletes are expert finders of flow. The reason is simple – another major flow trigger is **<u>risk</u>**.

Extreme athletes are professional risk-takers. And what does high-consequence risk do?

It drives focus.

By now you're beginning to see why one might consider swallowing swords. Or at least, why I might.

From a young age, complexity, challenge, and the risk involved in an unstable home life forced my focus into deep study. This was my first taste of these optimal states of consciousness. My situation forced me into flow, where **I discovered the possibility of my own potential**.

Over time, I realized shortcuts to achieve the flow state through risk-based activities, so I focused on increasing my skill so that I could increase my risk in an effort to drive focus.

First were the youthful activities, as varied as cliff jumping to juggling, skateboarding to tree climbing. Later, those activities began to migrate toward fire walking, fire eating, skydiving, and ultimately to what felt like the greatest risk – public speaking.

As skill increases, it's necessary to continue ratcheting up the challenge in order to find progressively more profound states of flow. That's how we end up with all of our greatest accomplishments, be they athletic, artistic, or intellectual.

Behind every innovation is a person in flow.

For me at the time, sword swallowing seemed to be the holy grail of mind-over-body stunts. The ultimate focus producer. Something I believed to be just on the edge of the impossible. A feat that would require me to stretch my skill just enough to potentially move over the line of reasonable. It was the next logical thing.

With sword swallowing, as with all high-risk endeavors, the choice is clear: **Flow or die.**

Flow is what I did.

Sword swallowing represents one of many steps on my own personal path to self-actualization. It has helped me to discover, push back, and ultimately shatter what I perceived my limitations to be. And it all started with one thing: focus.

Again:

Risk drives focus. Flow follows focus. Increase risk (with attendant increase in skill) and you increase flow.

These days, the actual act of swallowing swords produces less flow than it once did. It's simply the nature of the beast. As skill and comfort increase and challenges decrease, access to flow through that specific modality grows more difficult.

Something has to change.

The skill-to-challenge ratio needs to be maintained, and in the face of growing skill, you need to seek larger challenge.

But be assured, it still produces plenty of focus!

NOW, WITH FOCUS

I continue on my personal journey of generating more peak experiences through other avenues, lately and most notably that of rock climbing, an activity that takes me around the world, in contact with the most profound landscapes, while simultaneously pulling more flow triggers than any of my endeavors to date.

Yet sword swallowing still plays a central role in all I do. It's a fantastic demonstration of what's possible when you're able to access these states, and it allows me to connect with diverse audiences all over the country. It starts the conversation, and once begun, I'm able to engage in my other passion – **educating people about these profound non-ordinary states of consciousness, teaching them how to access them (without taking the risks I take!), and thereby live remarkable lives of achievement, well-being, and purpose.**

I guess you could call me a flow facilitator.

So in a sense, I'm still living that childhood dream of being an explorer. Perhaps I'm exploring more of the inner-space rather than outer-space. More of a psychonaut instead of an astronaut. Where my early choices were to go high into space or deep in a submarine, I suppose I've found a way to go both high and deep at the same time. And it's been one hell of a ride.

I hope you'll join me.

WORKS CITED

1. Maslow, A.H. (1964). Religions, values, and peak experiences. London: Penguin Books Limited.

2. Maslow, A. H. (1962). Toward a psychology of being. Princeton, NJ: Van Nostrand-Reinhold.

3. Csikszentmihalyi, Mihaly (1990). Flow: The Psychology of Optimal Experience. New York: Harper and Row.

4. Cranston, S. & Keller, S. (2013, January). Increasing the 'meaning quotient' of work. McKinsey Quarterly. Retrieved from: http://www.mckinsey.com/business-functions/organization/our-insights/increasing-the-meaning-quotient-of-work

5. Kotler, S., & Wheal, J. (2017). Stealing fire. New York, NY: Dey St., an imprint of William Morrow.

6. Kotler, S., & Wheal, J. (2017). Stealing fire.

A QUICK LI'L DITTY
ABOUT THE CONTRIBUTOR

Roderick Russell

Professional speaker,

sword swallower,

hypnotist,

mind-reader,

and climber.

Purveyor of the extraordinary,

exploring the intersection of

fear, focus, and flow.

Learn more: **RoderickRussell.com**

Radiate [rey-dee-eyt]

verb (used without object), radiated, radiating.

1. to extend, spread, or move like rays or radii from a center.
2. to emit rays, as of light or heat; irradiate.
3. to issue or proceed in rays.
4. (of persons) to project or glow with cheerfulness, joy, etc.: *She simply radiates with good humor.*

verb (used with object), radiated, radiating.

5. to emit in rays; disseminate, as from a center.
6. (of persons) to project (joy, goodwill, etc.).

CHAPTER 8

RADIATE

BY LANI VOIVOD

I should warn you: My friends call me **Boom Boom**.

And now I will warn you for a second time, because I just lied to you. My friends do not, in fact, call me Boom Boom. I wish they did, but it's a nickname I gave myself years ago, and it has never, EVER caught on. I've tried it on email signatures, biz networking nametags, tax documents, birth certificates, and more, but alas, no dice, no takers, no Boom Boom.

However, I find it incredibly relevant here, at the springboard of this essay. It's important you know someone self-dubbed as Boom Boom is about to launch into a maniacal thesis on dynamic energy, explosive ideas, transformational influence, cellular complexity, and, dare I say, **a spiritual and metaphysical call to arms**.

TRUTH BE TOLD

When I first chose the word **RADIATE** as my jam – my official workshop theme word – for the fourth iteration of the Live in Love Retreat, I chose it for two reasons:

1)   My fellow co-founders and I were having our #LILNH Retreat Kickoff Meeting, and while brainstorming the overarching vision, our suggestions were all ending in –ATE. Our dorky excitement about the prospect of rhyming our individual theme words this year sealed the deal.

2)   I hear myself saying **RADIATE** a lot while teaching my weekly yoga classes, as I guide students (and myself) through twists and postures, stretches and poses. The word always arises from the inside out, and it *always* feels quite lovely; like some ethereal combination of sunbeams, blue skies, butterfly kisses on Christmas morning, adorable puppy licks, and perspiration gleaned from Julie Andrews' frock in *The Sound of Music*.

Thus, like so many of life's most meaningful and fate-laden gifts, I hadn't realized **RADIATE**'s full **symphony of synchronicities** until I mindfully, purposefully sat myself down to marinate in them.

It's this radiant symphony I'm joyfully jonesing to share with you.

BUT FIRST, ALLOW ME TO COMMIT CRIMES AGAINST THE SCRUPULOUSNESS AND SANCTITY OF SCIENCE

While I would like to pretend to have several advanced degrees in physics, biology, chemistry, theology, physiology, technology, and nuclear energy as they pertain to the art and act of radiation, I'll do us both a favor and assume you're hip enough to call my bluff. Instead, I'll politely ask to take a few creative liberties, specifically inviting the virtues of brevity and enthusiasm to replace those of careful, clean, sense-making science.

So here are **ten brain-tickling, hacked-up info blurbs**. Sit back, relax, and simply take them in. (Don't worry - there will be no quiz at the end of this chapter.)

1. In physics, radiation is understood as **the emission or transmission of energy** in the form of waves or particles through space or matter.

2. The *Encyclopedia Britannica* website talks about how **"all matter is constantly bombarded with radiation"** from both cosmic and terrestrial sources, and goes on to say: **"Considerable attention is devoted to the consequences of such an energy transfer to living matter."**

3. In biology, radiation refers to **divergence out from a central point**, in particular *evolution* from an ancestral animal or plant group into a variety of new forms.

4. Ionizing radiation is generally bad for living things because **it**

packs a lot of heat and breaks chemical bonds; though this is pretty handy when it's used as a cancer treatment.

5. Non-ionizing radiation is generally fine, and includes **radio waves, microwaves, and light waves**.

6. **All modern communication systems use forms of electromagnetic radiation**; all objects give out and take in thermal radiation – aka infrared radiation – a type of electromagnetic radiation.

7. Some surfaces are better than others at **reflecting and absorbing** infrared radiation.

8. Scientists can **determine the composition of a substance** by studying the radiation it emits.

9. There's observable matter (atoms and molecules), the particles that constitute them (protons, electrons, and neutrons), and other elementary particles, dutifully forming the fabric of nature. **When a particle or group of particles is <u>accelerated</u>, it can reach high energies and travel a large distance in a very short time.**

10. According to NAP.edu (that's the website for the National Academies of Sciences, Engineering, and Medicine, for those who don't wear pocket protectors or have posters of Stephen Hawking and Marie Curie hanging on their beaker cabinets), radiation can be defined as **"any collection of elementary particles that have sufficient energy to interact with and transfer some of their**

energy to objects or materials that intercept their path."

There's also **acoustic** radiation, **gravitational** radiation, **solar** radiation, **nuclear** radiation, **Your Mom** radiation ... just kidding on that last one, but the list appears to go on and on.

What I'd like to focus on is the **indisputable power, scope, and impact** of these ideas in general, and borrow the fancy-pants science of them to buttress the Guest of Honor of our next conversation:

YOU.

YOUR LIGHT. YOUR HEAT. YOUR GLORIOUS, VICTORIOUS ENERGY!

Have you ever wondered why we can feel the heat of the sun, even though the life-giving fireball is 93 million miles away from Earth?

Prepare to be SHOCKED. The answer is – drumroll, please! – **radiation**.

This is where the aforementioned info blurbs come into play.

Unlike the transference of heat and energy via conduction, which involves direct contact between two or more objects to change the temp, the sun's energy abides by **the science of radiation**. The sun radiates most of its light and heat via visible wavelengths, and this type of energy travels *through space or matter*. (It can even travel through a vacuum, for that matter!)

These SUN-sational rays spur weather systems, beget photosynthesis, and ultimately, support and enable life as we know it.

And yet...

The sun is just one tiny, twinkling star among more than 100 billion in the Milky Way galaxy. Some scientists toss around the estimate of 10 trillion galaxies in the "observable universe." Our fabulous, fiery ball of glowing gases – at its core burning at about 27 million degrees Fahrenheit – is EVERYTHING to us. Us, the adorable, fumbling busybodies watching Netflix, drinking lattes, shopping in stores, fighting wars, and making YouTube videos, love, and blanket forts on Planet Earth.

The sun is not unlike **YOU**.

You. Total energy. A dynamic, evolving, energetic being. A miraculous, biological power source, as well as a co-creative, self-aware, ultra-kinetic source of singular, spectacular power.

You, just one of billions, and yet, **positively unique** in profoundly important ways.

You, with vital, life-giving brilliance at your core, generating your own electromagnetic fields, effortlessly transmitting your own heat and life through space and time, air and matter.

You may be just one out of many, but **you are EVERYTHING to some**, whether you know it or they know it, or not.

And you know what the coolest part is??!!

All of this is happening by science and design, without the help of your ego, opinions, plans, priorities, or financial assistance!

Do you see? Can you feel it? Are you beginning to grasp the magnitude here?

You are already scientifically designed to successfully radiate your light and energy to your ever-changing, infinitely expanding, instinctively collaborative universe.

So definitely, congrats on that, right?

Now, if you like the sound of that Ninja-esque skillset and are curious about taking it to the next level, hop onto your donkey and follow me, amigo!

HOW TO RADIATE LIKE A BOSS

First, you have to treat this built-in, wildly accessible and thrillingly nimble superpower with the faith and respect it deserves.

You don't walk around terrified, grabbing at trees and railings and other grounded objects because you're afraid gravity is a fickle force, do you? Then don't try to dissect and critique the nuances of molecular biology and astrophysics here.

You are energy. BOOM.

You are a conscious, creative being. BOOM.

You now have the choice to be a _consciously evolving_ creative being.

Can I get a BOOM BOOM??!!!

(See what I did there? Boom Boom or bust!)

You simply have to follow a few perky, painless guidelines.

1. HARNESS THE POWER OF INTENTION

You've probably heard spiritual leaders, healing communities, and at least a few of your Facebook friends yammering about the benefits of meditation, yoga, walking in nature, chillin' in float tanks, or just becoming more aware of your breath throughout the day. This is all part of honing and honoring the mind-body connection.

As we become more mindful of who we are, how we operate, and how we could (and perhaps should) wield our energy in this world, we begin to realize the game isn't all willy nilly after all.

We can learn powerful, proven ways to read, understand, and affect the playing field.

We can train the mind to CALM THE HECK DOWN ALREADY,

and align WITH the intuitive intelligence of the heart.

Eventually, we can allow the heart – the place where compassion, gratitude, personal truth, LOVE, generosity, joy, and **radiance** live - to grab the reins and take on the leadership role.

We can do all this and more, as long as we're aware, resilient, and willing.

2. FIND, ASSEMBLE, NURTURE, AND WORSHIP YOUR VERY OWN ITTY BITTY GIDDY COMMITTEE

Like it says in #7 of the info blurbs, some surfaces are better than others at reflecting and absorbing radiation. Similarly, some PEOPLE are better at reflecting and absorbing your particular brand of glow.

If you don't already know who these people are in your life, hunt them down. This is your quest. You are looking for the people who, more often than not, give you the experience of **GIDDY**.

I'm not necessarily saying they make you chortle-snort at your Aunt Edna's memorial service, or start whacking your face with a rubber chicken while singing *Camptown Races*. (Though they may do either or both.)

I *am* saying these magnificent mortals, these dazzling dynamos are vibrationally attuned to your dreams, values, and frequency.

The GIDDY is the raw, organic feeling of your subtle energy systems saying: "Yes! We're a match! We jibe! We have mysteries to explore together! We must mingle! We must dance! **WE ... MUST ... PLAY!**"

Your Itty Bitty Giddy Committee, this strategic team of radiant allies, doesn't have to know each other, though eventually one or all of them will probably meet. The important thing is for YOU to identify them, to treat them with the utmost respect and reverence, and to let them know they're an integral part of your Intentional Radiance aspirations.

If you *think* you know who they are but are getting resistance from them, or the relationship feels heavy or forced or boring or mediocre, let them go. Yeah, you can have them in your life, catch a movie together, exchange recipes, watch them Whip/Nae Nae, etc., but know they're *not* a card-carrying member of your IBGC. They might become one someday, but you guys aren't vibing like that yet. It's okay. All in good time.

Just follow the GIDDY. It's your IBGC GPS. It's real, it's fun, it's foolproof. Trust it and use it!

3. TAKE ADVANTAGE OF TECHNOLOGIES FOR INTENTIONAL RADIANCE

Okay, so you're tuned in to your radiant core. You're willing and downright psyched about reaching other people and communities with your cleaned-up, mindfully positive, empowering, heart-fueled light, love, and energy.

Yes, you can definitely, definitely join the Monks who chant on mountain tops and create measurable, healing shifts in the brain matter of patients and volunteers hooked up to EKG machines half way around the world. Totally rad if you did!

You can also use the incredibly accessible and socially ubiquitous tools of communication to reach across time and space to share your particular flavor of luminosity.

If you're reading this, odds are you aren't a rebellious teenager taking and sending risqué peekaboo pics to your closest 137 friends. My bet is you're beginning to get – or already have – a pretty good sense of who you are, what your gifts are, and how you *might* be able to use them to positively affect, enhance, inspire, or instigate at least a few people (or maybe even a few thousand people!) in your social network.

All you have to do to **begin reaching more people and influencing more lives with your judiciously directed energy core** is use one or some of our world's incredible communication platforms. With social media, mobile technology, texting, videos, livestreaming, and even far-out tech like holograms, 4D printers, and virtual reality systems, there's *virtually no limit* to sharing the stirrings of your heart and soul with others longing to connect with your vibrational moxie.

Ahhhh, but you don't love the idea of "putting yourself out there," do you? Believe it or not, most of us don't.

For most of us, the thought of radiating our hearts out to a broader spectrum of carbon-rich meat suits – and doing it WITH (gulp!) PURPOSE! – is about four clicks behind getting a root canal from an inebriated mall cop.

And even if we get over that first level of fear, the logistics of being media-ready are not always easy to navigate.

We may discover that good lighting and good hair days are few and far between. We might find out our tongues turn into floppy lumps of stuttering futility when we're trying to communicate the songs in our hearts and the fires in our souls. And we will definitely, eventually learn that the online trolls we fear will hurt our feelings with stupid yet cowardly comments.

Hopefully, though, we will be reminded of info blurb #3 — that when it comes to biology, radiation refers to *divergence out from a central point*. In this context, this central point is US, you and me.

Our DNA-deep duty, then, is to **muster the vision and courage to flow with our evolutionary instincts** — to kick into high gear our innate drive to willfully expand our thinking, energy field, and influence. This is the path to new realms of possibility and new levels of human consciousness.

OUR RADIANT BATTLE CRY

We must **REALIZE** our power, focus on our light, and become fierce in our intentionality.

We must **TRUST** in the energetic science of our efforts, understanding that the effects of our directed actions may not be immediately — or ever! — visible to the naked eye, yet are profound and powerful nonetheless.

We must **BELIEVE**, with all our hearts, in our conscious collaboration with an intelligent, benevolent universe.

Such connecting of the dots might indeed make us VERY giddy — enough for us to get over our wee human hang-ups, summon our best intentions, rally our Itty Bitty Giddy Committees, and **radiate** right into our brilliant and beckoning destinies.

Wishing you love, light, and infinite radiance,
Boom Boom

A QUICK LI'L DITTY

ABOUT THE CONTRIBUTOR

Lani Voivod

Mom, yoga teacher,

maniacal laughter addict.

Speaker,

social storyteller,

professional muse:

Epiphanies, Inc.

Creator:

31 Days of Possibility,

Live in Love Playbook,

Live in Love Fatebook.

Learn more: **LaniVoivod.com**

Activate [ak-tuh-veyt]

verb (used with object), activated, activating.

1. to make active; cause to function or act.
2. *Physics.*
    a. to render more reactive; excite:
        to activate a molecule.
    b. to induce radioactivity.
3. to aerate (sewage) in order to accelerate decomposition of impure organic matter by microorganisms.
4. *Chemistry.*
    a. to make (carbon, a catalyst, molecules, etc.) more active.
    b. to hasten (reactions) by various means, as heating.
5. to place (a military unit or station) on an active status in an assigned capacity.

CHAPTER 9

3...2...1...

ACTIVATE!

BY LANI VOIVOD

In the immortal words of Joey Tribbiani:

"How YOU doin'?"

If you read this book like I've been known to binge-watch *Game of Thrones*, you may feel a wee bit wonky.

After all, you just plowed through a lot of different voices! A cacophony of insights! A gauntlet-throwing deluge of dares, recommendations, riffs, and ideologies!

If, on the other hand, you took a more meandering approach – leafing lazily through chapters, skipping around here and there, flirting with the pages whenever the muse calls, soaking it in over the course of weeks, months, or years – you may feel chill as a cucumber on a Rockefeller party platter.

Whatever your station or circumstance, **check in with yourself** ...

And if you're feeling reeeeaaallly brave and bold, ask and answer these questions:

- What's bubbling up to the forefront of your mind?

- What's brewing behind your consciousness curtain?

- Are you thinking about anyone, any thing, or any place?

- Do you notice any fuzzy memories coming into focus?

- Forgotten dreams tugging at corners of your mind?

- Prickly sensations popping up anywhere in the body?

- Are you inspired to sit in stillness, call an old friend, or Google an old flame?

- Are you unbelievably sleeeeeeeeeeepy?

- Or are you ready to climb a mountain, write a book, launch a business, or go dancing 'til the break of dawn?

Tune into these questions. Allow answers to arise.

Jot down some of your responses, sketch or doodle them, or better yet, journal them out in a fevered frenzy.

Most importantly, **<u>PAY ATTENTION</u>**.

Pay attention to the **resistance or excitement** you feel.

Pay attention to the **chattering commentary** in your brain.

Pay attention to the **compassionate whispers** from your heart.

Tune into these questions. Allow answers to arise.

Will you allow yourself to be the **curious witness** to the stirrings of your soul?

Please, please, please, say, **"Yes."**

ACTIVATING THE VORTEX OF NOW

Step into the magical, mystical, all-powerful vortex of **NOW**.

Use **breath, faith,** and **focus** to let go of the niggling fear critters that distract you from knowing your next micro action, or from taking your next quantum leap.

You don't need them any more. They don't serve you. You're on to their silly little games, and guess what? You can *choose* not to play them. Not today, not tomorrow, and not ever again.

Instead, you have chosen to:

- **Validate** your dreams, power, and purpose
- **Resonate** with your creative instincts
- **Communicate** your sacred truth
- **Appreciate** your personal journey
- **Liberate** your mind from limiting beliefs
- **Concentrate** on your unique skills and deep-seated potential
- **Radiate** your levity, light, and love

And we thank you! We thank you! Oh boy, do we thank you!!!

Why do we care so deeply?

Because, while you are just one person out of billions on this third rock from the sun, you are *everything* – EVERYTHING! – to some beautiful, wonderful, ordinary and extraordinary people.

Some of these people you may know intimately. Others may be casual acquaintances. Still others you have yet to meet.

Whatever your current relationship with these charming souls, they need you to do your life work. They need you to care – to go right into that flippin' psychic and spiritual arena, fight your demons, meet your mettle, and claim your Warrior Birthrights.

They need you to do this so they can follow your lead, and experience the transformational *oomph* of your divine light.

Ultimately, they need you to ACTIVATE your superpowers so they might learn how to trigger their own.

After all, this IS a connected, mysterious, hyper-collaborative universe, right?

You got this.

Now go forth, **live in love**, and make some magic!

Made in the USA
Columbia, SC
20 March 2018